DRAWING CHIBI PETS

LEARN TO DRAW
KAWAII COMPANIONS
FROM DOGS, CATS, AND HAMSTERS
TO LIZARDS AND FISH!

Illustrations by Tessa Creative Art
Text by Oriel Voegele

ULYSSES BOOKS
FOR YOUNG READERS

Published by:
Ulysses Books for Young Readers
an imprint of Ulysses Press
PO Box 3440
Berkeley, CA 94703
www.ulyssespress.com

ISBN: 978-1-64604-792-5
Library of Congress Control Number: 2024944975

Printed in Canada
10 9 8 7 6 5 4 3 2 1

Acquisitions editor: Shelona Belfon
Managing editor: Claire Chun
Editor: Anna Embree
Proofreader: Paula Dragosh
Artwork: Tessa Creative Art
Layout: Winnie Liu

CONTENTS

FURRY & FEATHERY

CAT

The cat is the purr-fect pet and cutest companion.

STEP 1 Draw a round head and sketch perpendicular lines intersecting at the bottom third of the shape. These lines will guide you in placing the cat's facial features.

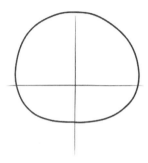

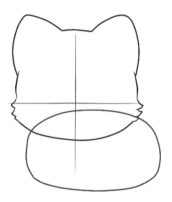

STEP 2 Sketch a slightly flattened oval body that overlaps the bottom of the head. Add two rounded triangle shapes at the top of the head for the cat's ears. To create a fur texture, draw mini triangles along the sides of the cat's face.

STEP 3 Add front paws by drawing a rounded W shape at the bottom left side of the body.

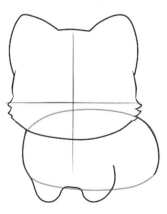

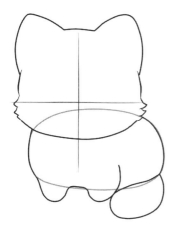

STEP 4 Sketch a curved tail at the bottom right side of the body.

STEP 5 Erase any overlapping lines. Add a patch of white chest fur by drawing a rounded shape between the two front paws.

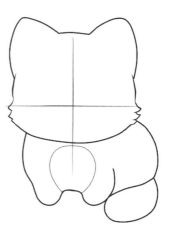

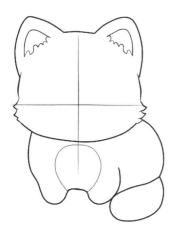

STEP 6 For the inner ears, draw two slightly rounded triangles with jagged bottoms.

STEP 7

Using the perpendicular lines as a guide, draw two big black circles for pupils. Create the white of the eye and eyelashes by drawing curved lines. Sketch a small curved eyebrow above each eye.

STEP 8

Erase the perpendicular lines. Draw the cat's nose with a rounded upside-down triangle and a rounded W shape. Add three curved lines for whiskers on each side of the face and a few white spots in the eyes for highlights.

Keep going from step 1.

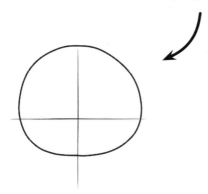

Try a few from scratch.

SHIBA INU

This sturdy dog breed is popular in Japan because of its foxlike appearance and confident personality.

STEP 1 Draw a round shape with a slightly widened bottom for the head. Draw perpendicular lines that are slightly curved to give your drawing a 3D effect. These lines will act as a guide for placing facial features.

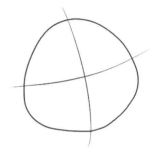

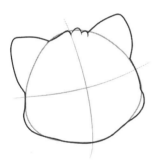

STEP 2 Draw two rounded triangle ears. Add tufts of fur at the top of the head by drawing a small rounded M shape. Enhance the cheeks with two curved lines on the sides of the Shiba Inu's face.

STEP 3 Sketch a slightly flattened oval body that overlaps with the bottom left quarter of the Shiba Inu's head. Draw two U-shaped lines on the bottom left side of the body for the hind legs.

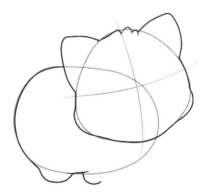

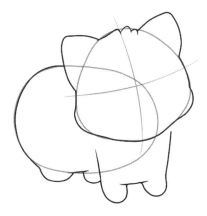

STEP 4

Add front legs by drawing two straight lines that curve at the bottom into rounded paws. Draw a short line between the paws to connect them to the Shiba Inu's torso.

STEP 5

Create a scarf. Draw a rounded line underneath the Shiba Inu's face to create the base of the scarf. Draw two curved shapes with smaller U-shaped lines inside of them at the left side of the Shiba Inu's face to create the ends of the scarf.

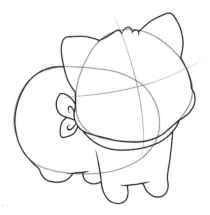

STEP 6

Using the perpendicular lines as a guide, add two black circles for eyes. Draw a curved line at the top left of the Shiba Inu's body to create a cute tail.

STEP 7

Draw two slightly rounded triangle shapes with bumpy bottoms to create the inner ears. Add the Shiba Inu's famous coat pattern with curved lines on the chest, body, and tail.

STEP 8

Erase any overlapping lines. Draw a curving line across the Shiba Inu's face to create its facial markings. Draw a small oval nose and three U-shaped lines for the mouth. Above each eye sketch ovals for bushy eyebrows and add white spots to each eye for highlights.

Keep going from step 1.

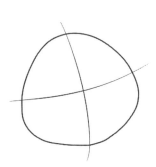

Try a few from scratch.

PARROT

The parrot is known for its colorful feathers, ability to mimic human speech, and affectionate personality.

STEP 1
Sketch a round head. Add perpendicular lines that are slightly curved to give your drawing a 3D effect. These lines will help in placing facial features.

STEP 2
Create the parrot's face by adding bumps along the sides of the head. Draw three long, curved feathers at the top of the head.

STEP 3
Draw a large oval body below the head. Add bumpy lines to give it a feathered texture.

STEP 4 Create a curved wing shape on the left side of the body with rows of bumpy lines for feathers.

STEP 5 Draw part of a wing on the right side of the body with the same bumpy line texture. Add two sets of three small rough ovals for the parrot's claws.

STEP 6 Using the perpendicular lines as a guide, add two black circles for eyes and two small curved eyebrows. Draw two parallel curving lines for a branch for the parrot to perch on.

STEP 7

Draw a large beak using two curved shapes. Add a few football-shaped leaves to the branch.

STEP 8

Sketch the parrot's long tail feathers below the left wing, partially hidden by the branch. Erase any overlapping lines. Draw branching lines within the leaves.

DRAWING CHIBI PETS

Keep going from step 1.

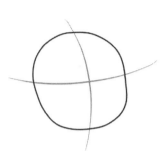

Try a few from scratch.

PARAKEET

The parakeet, also known as a budgie, is a small, friendly bird. Parakeets are easy to care for and an ideal pet choice for many beginning bird enthusiasts.

STEP 1 Draw a round head and create perpendicular lines that are slightly curved for a 3D effect. These lines will act as a guide for placing facial features.

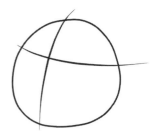

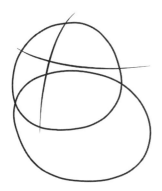

STEP 2 Draw a slightly oval body that overlaps with the bottom half of the head.

STEP 3 Using the perpendicular lines as a guide, add two black circles for eyes. Sketch a few curved lines on the top and bottom of the parakeet's head to create a feather texture.

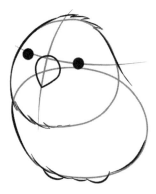

STEP 4 Draw a simple upside-down tear-drop shape for the beak. Add curved lines at the bottom of the parakeet's body to depict feathers.

STEP 5 Draw an oval on the right side of the parakeet's body to make a wing. Add the same feather texture from step 3 to the bottom of the wing.

STEP 6 Erase the perpendicular lines from step 1. Sketch a tail on the bottom right side of the body by drawing three long thin bumps.

STEP 7

Add the parakeet's claws by drawing two curved lines that each connect to three small bumps for the toes.

STEP 8

Erase any remaining overlapping lines. Draw a branch for the parakeet to perch on by drawing two curved lines. Add football-shaped leaves to the ends of the branch. Draw branching lines within the leaves.

DRAWING CHIBI PETS

Keep going from step 1.

Try a few from scratch.

HAMSTER

The hamster is a cute, cuddly pet that is small enough to fit in the palm of your hand.

STEP 1 Sketch a slightly flattened round head. Draw perpendicular lines that are slightly curved to give your drawing a 3D effect. These lines will act as a guide for placing facial features.

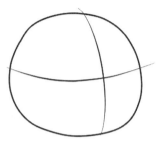

STEP 2 Create the hamster's face shape. Slightly erase the bottom of the head. Draw a straight line on the top left side of the head and a curved line on the bottom right side.

STEP 3 Draw a large round body. Add two upside-down U-shaped ears and two smaller upside-down U shapes for the inner ears.

STEP 4

Lighten the line where the body overlaps with the head. Add a few curved lines at the bottom of the body.

STEP 5

Completely erase the line where the body overlaps with the head. Add two small oval feet.

STEP 6

Draw two upside-down U-shaped arms. Add a circle for the white fur patch on the hamster's belly. Sketch a squiggly line for the fur pattern on the hamster's head.

STEP 7

Using the perpendicular lines as a guide, add two black circles for eyes and two small curved eyebrows.

STEP 8

Erase any remaining overlapping lines. Draw a small rounded upside-down triangle nose with a short vertical line coming off the bottom. Add white spots to each eye for highlights.

Sketch a few more!

Keep going from step 1.

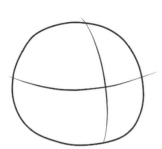

Try a few from scratch.

DRAWING CHIBI PETS

GUINEA PIG

An animal with a big personality and an even bigger heart, the guinea pig is a charming, easy-to-care-for companion.

STEP 1 Sketch a slightly flattened round head. Draw perpendicular lines that intersect at the top third of the head, curving slightly for a 3D effect. These lines will guide the placement of facial features.

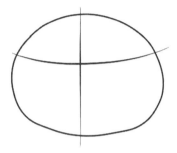

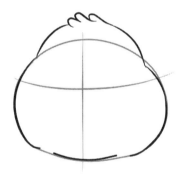

STEP 2 Add a curved shape with three small bumps at the top of the head.

STEP 3 Lightly sketch a slightly flattened round body overlapping the right half of the head. Add two U-shaped ears to both sides of the new top of the head.

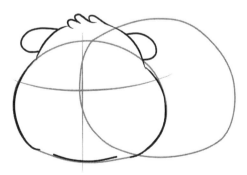

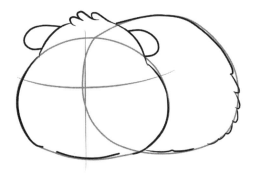

STEP 4 Draw a bumpy line around the back of the body to create a fur texture.

STEP 5 Erase any overlapping lines. Add three small oval feet.

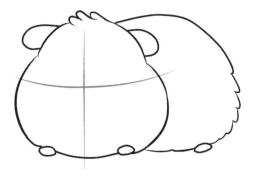

STEP 6 Using the perpendicular lines as a guide, add two circles for eyes and two small curved eyebrows.

STEP 7

Draw a small rounded upside-down triangle nose above a rounded W-shaped mouth.

STEP 8

Add white spots to each eye for highlights. Sketch two curved lines to create the fur pattern around the eyes. Add curved bumpy lines for the fur pattern on the body.

DRAWING CHIBI PETS

Keep going from step 1.

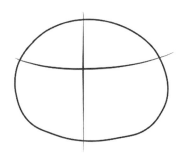

Try a few from scratch.

RABBIT

The rabbit hops to the top of the list of cutest animals because of its long ears, big eyes, and twitchy nose.

STEP 1 Draw a round head. Create perpendicular lines that are slightly curved to give your drawing a 3D effect. These lines will act as a guide for placing facial features.

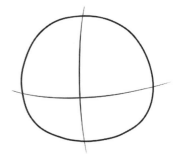

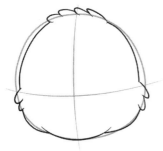

STEP 2 Add fur texture by sketching thin bumps on the cheeks and the top of the rabbit's head.

STEP 3 Draw the famous rabbit ears as two elongated upside-down U shapes at the top of the head.

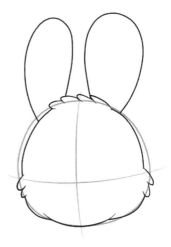

STEP 4 Draw the rabbit's torso and front legs. Sketch a bumpy curved line that turns into wide, rounded U-shaped feet connected by a straight line.

STEP 5 Complete the rabbit's body by adding a round shape with some jagged bumps for fur to the right of the torso.

STEP 6 Using the perpendicular lines as a guide, add two black circles for eyes and two small curved eyebrows. Draw a small rounded upside-down triangle nose with a short vertical line coming off the bottom. Sketch the rabbit's fluffy tail by drawing a few curved lines at the bottom right of the body.

STEP 7 Create the rabbit's inner ears with two smaller elongated upside-down U shapes. Add a white spot to each eye for a highlight.

STEP 8 Erase any overlapping lines.

Keep going from step 1.

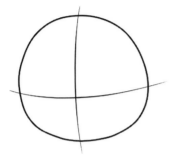

Try a few from scratch.

DRAWING CHIBI PETS

DUST BUNNY

Dust bunnies are small clumps of dust that form under furniture. You won't want to sweep away this cute chibi version!

STEP 1 Sketch a slightly flattened, round head. Add slightly curved perpendicular lines as a guide for placing facial features.

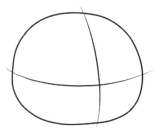

STEP 2 Create the dust bunny's texture with curved cloudlike lines around the head.

STEP 3 Add two cloudlike bunny ears, with the right ear bending over.

STEP 4 Sketch two round cloudlike feet below the head.

STEP 5 Add a larger cloudlike body to the left of the head.

STEP 6 Add a small cloudlike tail to the top left side of the body.

STEP 7

Draw two black circles for eyes and two small curved eyebrows.

STEP 8

Erase any overlapping lines. Draw a rounded upside-down triangle nose and a rounded W-shaped mouth. Add a white spot to each eye for a highlight.

DRAWING CHIBI PETS

Sketch a few more!

Keep going from step 1.

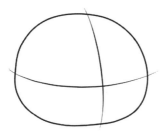

Try a few from scratch.

GOAT

Goats are fun, social creatures that love to bleat for extra love and attention.

STEP 1 Draw a slightly flattened round head. Draw an oval body that overlaps the bottom left corner of the head.

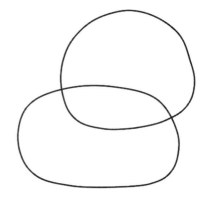

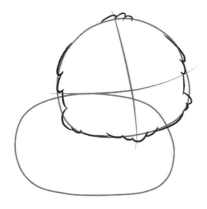

STEP 2 Create perpendicular lines that are slightly curved to give your drawing a 3D effect. These lines will help you position facial features. Add the goat's fur texture to the head. Create bumps at the top of the head, the bottom of the chin, and both sides of the face.

STEP 3 Add two upside-down U-shaped ears at the top corners of the head.

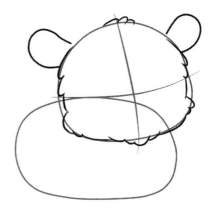

STEP 4

Add fur texture to the oval body. Create two rounded triangles for horns at the top of the head between the goat's ears.

STEP 5

Draw three curved parallel lines inside each horn. Sketch the goat's chest fur by drawing a bumpy rounded triangle underneath the head.

STEP 6

Using the perpendicular lines as a guide, draw two black circles for eyes and two small curved eyebrows. Add four U-shaped legs.

STEP 7

Draw a rounded upside-down triangle for a nose. Sketch a fluffy tail at the top left corner of the body. Add two smaller upside-down U shapes for the inner ears.

STEP 8

Erase any overlapping lines. Add white spots to each eye for highlights and draw a rounded W-shaped smile.

Keep going from step 1.

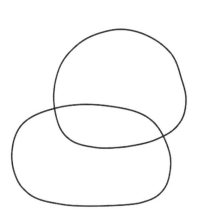

Try a few from scratch.

CHINCHILLA

Known for being beautiful and a bit shy, chinchillas are the introverts of the rodent world.

STEP 1 Draw a round shape with a slightly wider bottom for the head. Add slightly curved perpendicular lines intersecting at the bottom third of the head to guide the placement of facial features.

STEP 2 Add a bumpy fur texture around the head.

STEP 3 Draw two large upside-down U-shaped ears. Lightly sketch a round body that overlaps the bottom left of the chinchilla's head.

STEP 4 Add bumpy fur texture to the back of the chinchilla's body. Draw a curved line for a hind foot and two smaller curved lines for toes.

STEP 5 Draw the two front legs. For each leg draw two curved lines connected to three U-shaped toes.

STEP 6 Using the perpendicular lines as a guide, add two black circles for eyes and two small curved eyebrows. Sketch a patch of chest fur by drawing a curved bumpy line above the front feet and connected to the chinchilla's face.

STEP 7

Draw two curved lines to create the chinchilla's inner ears and add a rounded, upside-down triangle nose.

STEP 8

Erase any overlapping lines. Draw two curved lines on both sides of the nose to create the chinchilla's whiskers and add white spots to each eye for highlights.

DRAWING CHIBI PETS

Keep going from step 1.

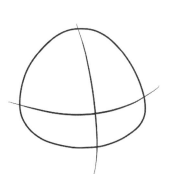

Try a few from scratch.

FERRET

Ferrets are playful animals that form strong bonds with their human owners.

STEP 1 Draw a small oval for the head. Add slightly curved perpendicular lines intersecting at the top third of the head as a guide for placing facial features.

STEP 2 Create the ferret's face shape. Draw sloping lines on each side of the head for cheeks. Add texture to the cheeks and draw bumps at the top of the head for the ears and fur.

STEP 3 Sketch the ferret's inner ear on the left by drawing a small semicircle with a jagged bottom. For the inner ear on the right, add a small curved line. Using the perpendicular lines as a guide, draw a rounded upside-down triangle for the nose above an upside-down V shape for the mouth.

STEP 4 Using the perpendicular lines as a guide, add two black ovals for eyes and two small curved eyebrows. Sketch the ferret's furry chest by drawing a small smooth curved line on the right and a longer jagged curved line on the left. Add jagged lines below the small curved line.

STEP 5
Elongate the body by drawing two more jagged lines. Add a white spot to each eye for a highlight.

STEP 6
Draw each of the ferret's front feet with two curved lines connected by three U-shaped toes. Add a small bumpy line above each set of toes.

STEP 7
Sketch each of the ferret's back feet with two curved lines connected by two or three U-shaped toes. Draw a few curved lines above the toes of the inner foot. Add a goggle shape around the ferret's eyes for its famous mask.

STEP 8
Draw the ferret's tail with two parallel lines in a backward C shape.

Keep going from step 1.

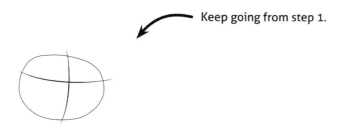

Try a few from scratch.

PONY

Despite being small, ponies are incredibly strong and able to pull loads over twice their weight!

STEP 1 Sketch an irregular bean-shaped head. Add slightly curved perpendicular lines as a guide for placing facial features.

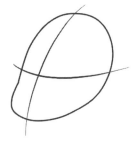

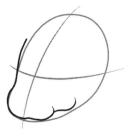

STEP 2 Create the pony's face shape by drawing a couple of curved lines at the bottom right side of the head.

STEP 3 Draw an oval-shaped body overlapping the bottom right corner of the head. Add two upside-down U-shaped ears to the top of the head. Give the ears a slight point at the tips.

STEP 4

Create the pony's mane with swooping curved lines between the ears on the forehead and on the right side of the head.

STEP 5

Using the perpendicular lines as a guide, add two black circles for eyes and two small curved eyebrows. Draw the pony's legs with a few curved lines at the bottom of the body, making the hind legs smaller than the front legs.

STEP 6

Erase some of the overlapping lines. Sketch the pony's tail with a few concentric curved lines on the right side of the body.

STEP 7

Add a small football-shaped inner ear on the right side. Draw a curved line on each of the three most visible legs to create hooves.

STEP 8

Erase any remaining overlapping lines. Draw the pony's muzzle with a curved line at the bottom left of the head and add two small upside-down U shapes for nostrils. Add white spots to each eye for highlights.

Keep going from step 1.

Try a few from scratch.

UNICORN

Known for its majestic horn and beautiful mane, the unicorn is a mythical creature that symbolizes innocence and power.

STEP 1 Sketch an irregular bean-shaped head. Draw perpendicular lines that are slightly curved to give your drawing a 3D effect. These lines will act as a guide for placing facial features.

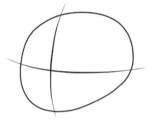

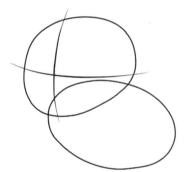

STEP 2 Draw an oval-shaped body that overlaps with the bottom right corner of the head.

STEP 3 Add an upside-down U-shaped ear on the top right side of the head. Give the ear a slight point at the tip. Create the unicorn's mane with a collection of swooping curved lines on the left, top, and right of the head.

STEP 4

Add the unicorn's legs by drawing four curved shapes, making the front legs larger than the hind legs.

STEP 5

Draw a football-shaped inner ear. Add curved lines within each leg to create hooves. On the right side of the body draw a round curved tail ending in a swirl.

STEP 6

Using the perpendicular lines as a guide, add two black circles for eyes and two small curved eyebrows. Create the unicorn's signature horn with an elongated triangle with a rounded bottom, detailing it with curved lines.

STEP 7

Sketch more swooping curved lines within the mane and tail to give your unicorn's hair more texture. Add two small upside-down U-shaped nostrils and a sideways U-shaped smile.

STEP 8

Erase any overlapping lines and add a few white spots to each eye for highlights.

Keep going from step 1.

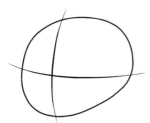

Try a few from scratch.

HEDGEHOG

Hedgehogs are famous for their prickly spines and ability to curl into a ball to protect themselves.

STEP 1 Draw a slightly flattened round head. Sketch perpendicular lines that are slightly curved to give your drawing a 3D effect. These lines will act as a guide for placing facial features.

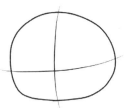

STEP 2 Sketch the hedgehog's left cheek with two curved lines.

STEP 3 Draw an oval body that slightly overlaps the bottom of the head. Add two small oval feet.

STEP 4 Draw two U-shaped arms and two upside-down U-shaped ears.

STEP 5

Using the perpendicular lines as a guide, add two black circles for eyes, two small curved eyebrows, and a small oval nose.

STEP 6

Sketch a large circle around the existing drawing. Draw a small rounded W-shaped mouth connected to the nose and two smaller upside-down U-shaped inner ears.

STEP 7

Add a jagged texture around the large circle, the hedgehog's forehead, and the right side of the inner body.

STEP 8

Erase any overlapping lines. Draw a curved line for the chest marking and add white spots to each eye for highlights. Sketch jagged lines within the large circle to create the hedgehog's famous spines.

Keep going from step 1.

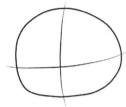

Try a few from scratch.

SCALY & AQUATIC

BEARDED DRAGON

The bearded dragon is a popular reptile pet because of its mild temperament.

STEP 1 Sketch a slightly flattened oval head. Add slightly curved perpendicular lines as a guide for facial features.

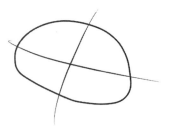

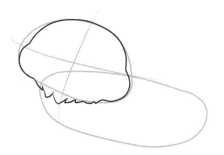

STEP 2 Create the bearded dragon's face shape by emphasizing the cheeks and drawing jagged details at the bottom of the head. Sketch a longer, flatter oval body that overlaps the bottom right corner of the head.

STEP 3 Add a few bumps to the bottom of the body.

STEP 4

Using the perpendicular lines as a guide, add two black circles for eyes and two small curved eyebrows. Sketch a curved tail at the top right of the body.

STEP 5

Add the bearded dragon's ruff around the head by creating a ring of inverted scallops.

STEP 6

Create the bearded dragon's legs with curved lines that connect to four round toes.

SCALY & AQUATIC

STEP 7 Add a wide rounded W-shaped mouth.

STEP 8 Erase any overlapping lines. Add white spots to each eye for highlights. Add texture to the bearded dragon's ruff with partially curved rectangular shapes that align with the inverted scallops. Sprinkle the bearded dragon's head and back with circles for markings.

Keep going from step 1.

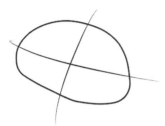

Try a few from scratch.

DRAGON

Dragons are mythical creatures believed by many cultures and legends to fly, breathe fire, and hoard riches.

STEP 1 Sketch a round head. Draw slightly curved perpendicular lines to give your drawing a 3D effect. These lines will act as a guide for placing facial features.

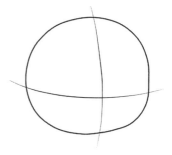

STEP 2 Sketch two cheek bumps on the bottom corners of the dragon's head.

STEP 3 Draw two curved, pointy ears at the top of the head.

STEP 4

Sketch the inner ears. The left inner ear ends in a squiggly line, and the right inner ear ends at the edge of the head. Below the head, add two curved front legs with slight indents on the inner sides.

STEP 5

Add two large circles for the outer edges of the dragon's eyes. Draw curved lines for the dragon's body and back legs.

STEP 6

Draw two curved lines within each eye circle to create the dragon's irises and pupils. Add two curved eyebrows and two curved nostrils. Create the dragon's horns with two rounded triangles at the top of the head. Connect the left horn to the left ear with a curved line. Add a curved tail to the left of the dragon's body using one solid line and one dashed line.

STEP 7

Add three round toes to the bottom of each leg. Between the dashed line sections on the tail draw rounded triangles for spikes. Add similar rounded triangle spikes to the left side and top of the dragon's head. Sketch two curved lines for the mouth and draw a curved line between the tops of the front legs to create the dragon's chest markings.

STEP 8

Color in the dragon's pupils and add white spots for highlights. Draw three curved lines on each of the horns and on the belly. Create a spiky fan shape at the end of the tail with inverted scallops and add triangles inside that align with the scallops. Use inverted scallops again to make batlike wings behind each shoulder. Fill in the wings with curved rectangular shapes that align with the scallops.

DRAWING CHIBI PETS

Keep going from step 1.

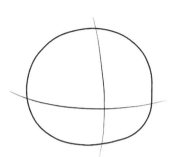

Try a few from scratch.

ROCK

A rock may just be a solid collection of minerals, but it also makes a great low-maintenance pet! There are three types of rocks: sedimentary, igneous, and metamorphic.

 Draw an irregular oval shape.

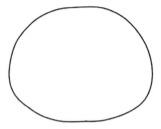

STEP 2 Draw perpendicular lines that are slightly curved to give your drawing a 3D effect.

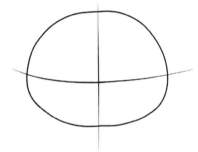

STEP 3 Make the rock edges rougher by drawing straight lines around the border of the oval.

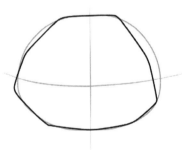

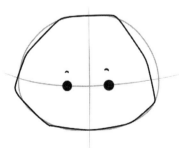

STEP 4 Add two black circles for eyes and small curved eyebrows.

STEP 5 Draw a rounded mouth.

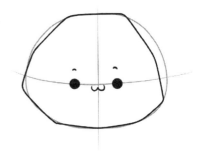

STEP 6 Erase any overlapping lines. Draw a large upside-down U shape around the face and add straight lines connecting it to the edge of the rock.

STEP 7 Add a group of three thin curved shapes to both sides of the rock for leaves.

 STEP 8 Draw branching lines within the leaves.

DRAWING CHIBI PETS

Keep going from step 1.

Try a few from scratch.

SEA MONKEY

Famous for hatching when its eggs are put in water, the sea monkey is a type of brine shrimp. This chibi version is an imaginative interpretation.

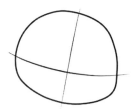

STEP 1 Draw a slightly flattened round head. Add slightly curved perpendicular lines for a 3D effect. These lines will act as a guide for placing facial features.

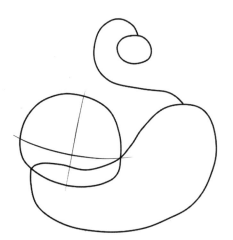

STEP 2 Draw a larger bean-shaped body that slightly overlaps the bottom of the head. At the top of the body sketch a squiggly line with a circle at the end.

STEP 3 Create the sea monkey's face shape by drawing curved cheeks on the bottom of the head and three small long bumps at the top. Sketch two curved lines the base of the sea monkey's tail.

STEP 4

Using the perpendicular lines as a guide, add two black circles for eyes and two small curved eyebrows. Add gills on both sides of the sea monkey's face by drawing two curved lines connected by three inverted scallops. Continue the tail by extending the curved lines of the tail base. Follow the squiggly line from step 2. At the end of the tail, draw three round bumps.

STEP 5

Add a small rounded upside-down triangle for a nose. Create three legs using curved lines connected by three to four bumps for toes.

STEP 6

Draw a wide rounded W-shaped smile. Add curved lines inside the top of the head for the sea monkey's facial markings.

STEP 7

Draw two curved lines across the bottom of the body to create the sea monkey's belly. Sketch a few curved lines inside the belly. Add texture to the gills with curved rectangular shapes that align with the scallops.

STEP 8

Erase any overlapping lines and add white spots to each eye for highlights. Draw scales on the body, back, and tail.

Keep going from step 1.

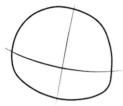

Try a few from scratch.

GECKO

Geckos are cute reptiles and popular pets. Fun fact: they can climb on walls!

STEP 1 Draw an oval for the head. Draw perpendicular lines that are slightly curved to give your drawing a 3D effect. These lines will act as a guide for placing facial features.

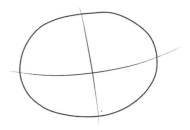

STEP 2 Create the gecko's face shape by sketching curved cheeks and two bumps at the top of the head.

STEP 3 Draw two short curved lines under the gecko's head and one longer curved line wrapping around the left side of the head.

STEP 4 Add the gecko's front legs. Each leg should have two curved lines that connect to three U-shaped toes.

STEP 5 Extend the long curved line from step 3 to create a tail that wraps around the gecko's head.

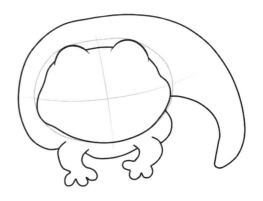

STEP 6 Using the perpendicular lines as a guide, add two black ovals for eyes and two small curved eyebrows. Draw a curved line under the chin for the gecko's belly marking. Draw another curved line on the tail to create depth.

STEP 7

Add a white spot to each eye for a highlight and draw two small lines for nostrils.

STEP 8

Erase any overlapping lines. Draw a wide rounded W-shaped mouth. Sprinkle the gecko's head, body, and tail with small circles for markings.

Keep going from step 1.

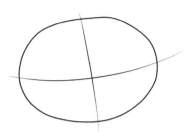

Try a few from scratch.

GOLDFISH

This famous freshwater fish is a popular pet, and while it might be called a goldfish, it comes in many different colors, including white, black, and orange.

STEP 1 Draw a round head. Create perpendicular lines that are slightly curved to give your drawing a 3D effect. These lines will help you position facial features.

STEP 2 Create the goldfish's face shape by drawing curved lines for cheeks. Sketch another round shape around the top right side of the head.

STEP 3 Draw two squiggly fins on each side of the goldfish's head.

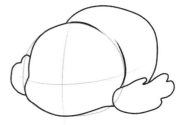

STEP 4 Add the top fin and the tail by drawing two squiggly shapes to the top left and to the right of the body.

STEP 5

Sketch a wide rounded W-shaped line across the bottom third of the goldfish's face. Add a scallop pattern to the body to create scales.

STEP 6

Draw two big circles for eyes and two small curved eyebrows. Add small circles at the top of the goldfish's head.

STEP 7

Draw curved lines on the goldfish's fins and tail for texture.

STEP 8

Erase any overlapping lines. Add a white spot to each eye for a highlight and draw a small U-shaped smile.

Keep going from step 1.

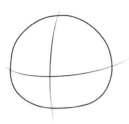

Try a few from scratch.

FROG

The world's favorite amphibian, frogs number over a thousand species and live in swamps, meadows, and even deserts.

STEP 1 Draw a slightly flattened oval for the head, adding slightly curved perpendicular lines intersecting near the top for a 3D effect.

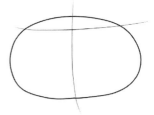

STEP 2 Create the frog's face shape by drawing a curved line for a cheek on either side of the head and two upside-down U shapes on top of the head for eye outlines.

STEP 3 Draw a flattened oval body underneath the frog's head, leaving two small gaps at the bottom for the frog's front legs.

STEP 4 Add two U-shaped front legs.

STEP 5 Sketch the frog's back legs. Draw a shape with one large round curve and one smaller flatter curve on both sides of the frog's lower body.

STEP 6 Draw two large black circles for eyes. Sketch an upside-down U shape for the chest marking and connect it to the tops of the front legs.

STEP 7 Scatter small circles on the frog's cheeks and body.

STEP 8 Add a white spot to each eye for a highlight. Erase any overlapping lines and draw a U-shaped mouth between the eyes.

Keep going from step 1.

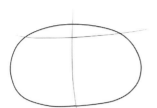

Try a few from scratch.

BETTA FISH

Betta fish are very attractive and hardy fish. Their vibrant color and beautiful fins make them a popular pet choice.

STEP 1 Draw a round head. Create perpendicular lines that are slightly curved to give your drawing a 3D effect. These lines will act as a guide for placing facial features.

STEP 2 Create a slightly flattened oval shape that overlaps with the top left corner of the head.

STEP 3 Darken select lines used to create the head and body.

STEP 4 Sketch two rounded squiggly fins.

STEP 5

Draw a large round shape as a guide for the tail.

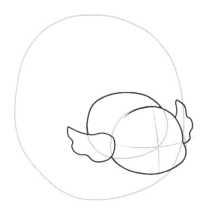

STEP 6

Using the perpendicular facial lines as a guide, add two black circles for eyes and two small curved eyebrows. Use the large round shape as a guide to sketch the betta fish's tail with a squiggly line. Sketch a third fin at the bottom right corner of the betta fish's head.

STEP 7

Draw another squiggly line around the inside of the tail. In each fin, draw a few curved lines for texture. Sketch a scallop pattern on the betta fish's body for scales. Add a small U-shaped mouth.

STEP 8

Erase any overlapping lines. Add curved lines to the tail in a fanlike pattern.

Keep going from step 1.

Try a few from scratch.

AXOLOTL

Aquatic salamanders with the ability to regrow body parts, axolotls (pronounced "ak·suh·laa·tls") make great low-maintenance, hypoallergenic pets!

STEP 1
Draw a round shape with a slightly widened bottom for the head. Draw perpendicular lines that are slightly curved to give your drawing a 3D effect. These lines will act as a guide for placing facial features.

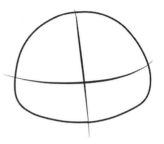

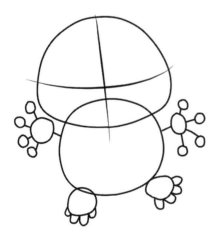

STEP 2
Draw a round body that slightly overlaps the bottom of the head. Create a guide for the axolotl's hands and feet. For each hand, draw a straight line that ends in a round shape. Off that round shape, draw four smaller straight lines that also end in round shapes to create the fingers. Draw the axolotl's feet as circles with four rounded toes.

STEP 3 Create the axolotl's face shape by adding two cheek bumps and a rounded chin.

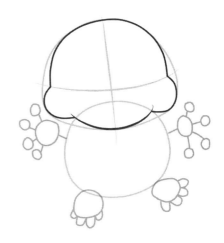

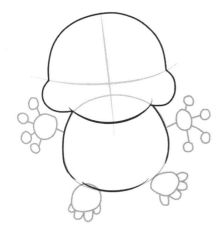

STEP 4 Darken the round body shape from step 2.

STEP 5 Using the perpendicular guide, add two black circles for eyes and two small curved eyebrows. Using the guide from step 2, draw the axolotl's hands.

STEP 6
Still using the guide from step 2, draw the axolotl's feet. Add curved lines for legs. Sketch a curved line to create a belly marking and draw a U-shaped smile.

STEP 7
Create three squiggly gills on both sides of the axolotl's head.

STEP 8
Erase any overlapping lines and add white spots to the eyes for highlights.

Keep going from step 1.

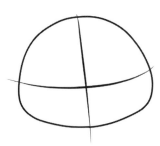

Try a few from scratch.

TURTLE

Turtles are known for their bony shells that protect them from predators.

STEP 1 Sketch a slightly flattened oval head. Draw perpendicular lines that are slightly curved to give your drawing a 3D effect. These lines will act as a guide for placing facial features.

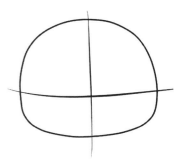

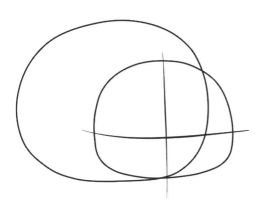

STEP 2 Draw a larger slightly flattened oval that overlaps most of the face.

STEP 3 Create the turtle's face shape. Draw two curved cheeks and a round forehead using the perpendicular lines as a guide.

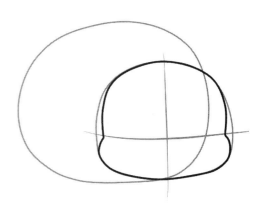

STEP 4

Sketch curved lines at the bottom of the large oval to create the bottom of the turtle's body.

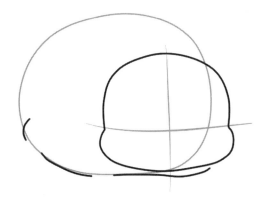

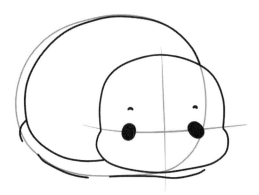

STEP 5

Using the perpendicular lines as a guide, add two black ovals for eyes and two small curved eyebrows. Create the turtle's shell by drawing a round shape that takes up most of the large oval.

STEP 6

Erase any overlapping lines and add a wide rounded W-shaped mouth.

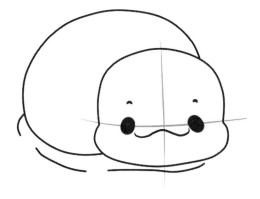

Create three rounded feet.

STEP 8 Draw the turtle's famous shell pattern by sketching polygonal shapes.

DRAWING CHIBI PETS

Keep going from step 1.

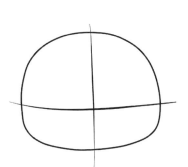

Try a few from scratch.

HERMIT CRAB

The hermit crab is a cute crustacean that searches for new shells to move into as it grows bigger.

STEP 1 Draw an oval head. Add slightly curved perpendicular lines for a 3D effect. These lines will act as a guide for placing facial features.

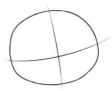

STEP 2 Create the hermit crab's face shape. Draw two curved cheeks and a round forehead using the perpendicular lines as a guide.

STEP 3 Again using the perpendicular lines as a guide, add two black ovals for eyes and two small curved eyebrows.

STEP 4 Add a rounded W shape for a mouth and a white spot to each eye for a highlight.

STEP 5   Sketch claws on both sides of the hermit crab's face with a big U shape connecting at the top to a curved V shape

STEP 6   Create the hermit crab's arms by drawing two U-shaped lines between the face and the claws on each side.

STEP 7   Sketch the base of the hermit crab's shell by drawing two large curved shapes. The line of the first curved shape connects to the claws. The second curved shape sits on top of the first.

STEP 8   Finish drawing the shell by creating two smaller curved shapes on top of the first two.

DRAWING CHIBI PETS

Keep going from step 1.

Try a few from scratch.

DRAWING CHIBI PETS

DRAWING CHIBI PETS

PRACTICE PAGE

Discover More Great How-to-Draw Books from Ulysses Press

Learn more at www.ulyssespress.com